bridges to
contemplative living
with thomas merton

four:
discovering the hidden ground of love

edited by jonathan montaldo & robert g. toth
of the merton institute for contemplative living

ave maria press AmP notre dame, indiana

Ave Maria Press acknowledges the permission of the following publishers for use of excerpts from these books:

"A Life Free from Care" by Thomas Merton. *Cistercian Quarterly* Vol 5.2, 1970. Used with permission of Cistercian Publications.

Conjectures of a Guilty Bystander by Thomas Merton, copyright © 1966 by the Abbey of Gethsemani. Used by permission of Doubleday, a division of Random House, Inc.

Jewels of Remembrance: A Daybook of Spiritual Guidance Containing 365 Selections From the Wisdom of Mevlâna Jalâluddin Rumi translated by Camille and Kabir Helminski, copyright © 2000. Reprinted by arrangement with Shambhala Publications, Inc. www.shambhala.com

Love and Living by Thomas Merton, copyright © 1979 by The Trustees of the Merton Legacy Trust. Used by permission of Harcourt Brace Jovanovich, Publishers

New Seeds of Contemplation, copyright © 1961 by The Abbey of Gethsemani. Reprinted by permission of New Directions Publishing Corp.

One Robe, One Bowl: The Zen of Ryokan, translated by John Stevens, copyright © 1977. Reprinted by arrangement with Shambhala Publications, Inc. www.shambhala.com

The Other Side of the Mountain: The Journals of Thomas Merton, Volume Seven 1967–1968 by Thomas Merton and edited by Patrick Hart, copyright © 1998 by The Merton Legacy Trust. Reprinted by permission of HarperCollins Publishers.

The Psalms, A New Translation, arranged by Joseph Gelineau, copyright © 1963 by Paulist Press, Inc. , New York, Mahwah, NJ. Used with permission. www.paulistpress.com.

The Roots of Christian Mysticism by Clément Olivier, copyright © 1993, New City Press. Reprinted with permission of New City Press.

A Search for Solitude: The Journals of Thomas Merton, Volume Three 1952–1960 by Thomas Merton and edited by Patrick Hart, copyright © 1996 by the Merton Legacy Trust. Preprinted by permission of HarperCollins Publishers.

Founded in 1865, Ave Maria Press is a ministry of the Indiana Province of Holy Cross.

www.avemariapress.com

ISBN-10 1-59471-091-0   ISBN-13 978-1-59471-091-9

Cover and text design by Andy Wagoner

Cover photograph © Robert Hill Photography

Interior photograph; Shops Building, Gethsemani, 1965, by Thomas Merton. Used with permission of the Merton Legacy Trust and the Thomas Merton Center at Bellarmine University. Interior photograph of Thomas Merton on p.7 by John Lyons. Used with permission of the Merton Legacy Trust.

Printed and bound in the United States of America.

B y being attentive, by learning to listen (or recovering the natural capacity to listen which cannot be learned any more than breathing), we can find ourselves engulfed in such happiness that it cannot be explained: the happiness of being at one with everything in that hidden ground of love for which there can be no explanations.

THOMAS MERTON
THE HIDDEN GROUND OF LOVE, 1985

A NOTE ABOUT INCLUSIVE LANGUAGE

Thomas Merton wrote at a time before inclusive language was common practice. In light of his inclusive position on so many issues and his references to our essential unity, we hope these texts will be read from an inclusive point of view.

CONTENTS

INTRODUCTION

WHAT DO WE MEAN BY CONTEMPLATIVE LIVING?

Life is a spiritual journey. Contemplative living is a way of responding to our everyday experiences by consciously attending to our relationships. It deepens the awareness of our connectedness and communion with others, becomes a positive force of change in our lives, and provides meaningful direction to our journey. Ultimately, contemplative living leads us to a sense of well-being, profound gratitude, and a clearer understanding of our purpose in life.

Living contemplatively begins with ourselves but leads us in the end to embrace deeply not only our truest self, but God, neighbor, and all of creation. By reflecting on our everyday experiences, we seek the depths of our inner truth. By exploring our beliefs, illusions, attitudes and assumptions, we find our true self and discover how we relate to the larger community. Contemplative living directs our minds and hearts to the truly important issues of human existence, making us less likely to be captivated by the superficial distractions that so easily occupy our time.

WHO WAS THOMAS MERTON?

For over fifty years, the thought and writings of Thomas Merton have guided spiritual seekers across the world. His writings offer important insights into four essential relationships—with self, with God, with other people, and with all of creation. While the Christian tradition is the foundation of his perspective, he is open and inclusive in his examination of other religious traditions, recognizing the important contribution that all faith traditions have made throughout the history of civilization. He draws from their strengths to enhance the spiritual growth of individuals and communities.

Thomas Merton was born in Prades, France, in 1915. His mother was from the United States and his father from New Zealand. Educated in France, England, and the United States, he received a master's degree in English from Columbia University. In 1938 he was baptized into the Catholic Church. He taught at St. Bonaventure University for a year and then in 1941 entered the Cistercian Order as a monk of the Abbey of Gethsemani in Kentucky. Directed by his Abbot, Dom Frederic Dunne, Merton wrote his autobiography, *The Seven Storey Mountain*, which was published in 1948.

For fifteen years he served as Master of Scholastics and Novices while writing many books and articles on the spiritual life, inter-religious understanding, peace, and social justice issues. In December of 1968, he journeyed to Asia to attend a conference of contemplatives near Bangkok, Thailand. While there he was accidentally electrocuted and died at the age of fifty-three.

Interest in Merton has grown steadily since his death. *The Seven Story Mountain* appears on lists of the one hundred most important books of the last century, has been in print ever since its first edition, and has sold millions of copies. The volume of printed work by and about him attests to Merton's popularity. His works have been translated into thirty-five languages and new foreign language editions continue to be printed. The International Thomas Merton Society currently has thirty chapters in the United States and fourteen in other countries.

Thomas Merton is distinguished among contemporary spiritual writers by the depth and substance of his thinking. Merton was a scholar who distilled the best thinking of the best theologians, philosophers, and poets throughout the centuries, from both the West and the East, and presented their ideas in the context of the Christian worldview. His remarkable and enduring popularity indicates that he speaks to the minds and hearts of people searching for answers to life's important questions. For many he is a spiritual guide, and for others he offers a place to retreat to in difficult times. His writings take people into deep places within themselves and offer insight into the paradoxes of life. They wrestle with how to be contemplative in a world of action, yet offer no quick fix or "Ten Easy Steps" to a successful spiritual life.

USING *BRIDGES TO CONTEMPLATIVE LIVING WITH THOMAS MERTON*

Bridges is intended for anyone seeking to live more contemplatively. For some it initiates a spiritual journey, for others it leads to re-examination or recovery of a neglected spiritual life, and for still others it deepens an already vibrant spirituality. Through reflection and dialogue on specific spiritual themes, participants revisit and refresh their perspectives on and understanding of life. They explore the strength and balance of the relationships that ultimately determine who they are: relationships with self, God, others, and nature. Through examining these relationships, participants probe their understanding of life's great questions:

"Who am I?"

"Who is God?"

"Why am I here?"

"What am I to do with my life?"

The selected readings move participants in and out of four dimensions of contemplative living—*Awakening* to an ever-deepening awareness of "true-self," *Contemplation* of a life experienced from a God-centered perspective, *Compassion* in relationships with others, and *Unity* realized in our undeniable and essential inter-connectedness with all of creation. This fourfold process of spiritual formation frames much of Merton's thought and writing.

This is not a spiritual formation program in some "other-worldly" sense. Merton insists that our spiritual life is our everyday lived experience. There is no separation between them. *Bridges* does not require an academic background in theology, religion, or spirituality, nor does it require use of any particular spiritual practices or prayers. There are no levels of perfection, goals to attain, or measurements of progress. This is not an academic or scholarly undertaking. Everyone will find a particular way of contemplative living within his or her own circumstances, religious tradition, and spiritual practices.

The *Bridges to Contemplative Living with Thomas Merton* series is especially designed for small group dialogue. The selected themes of each session are intended to progressively inform and deepen the relationships that form our everyday lives. Each session begins with scripture and ends in prayer. In between there are time and mental space for spiritual reading, reflection, and contemplative dialogue.

WHAT DO WE MEAN BY CONTEMPLATIVE DIALOGUE?

Contemplative dialogue is meant to be non-threatening, a "safe place" for open sharing and discussion. It is not outcome-oriented. It's not even about fully understanding or comprehending what one reads or hears from the other participants. The focus is on *listening* rather than thinking about how we will respond to what we hear. Simply hearing and accepting another's point of view and reflecting on it can inform and enlighten our own perspective in a way that debating or analyzing it cannot. The pace of conversation is slower in contemplative dialogue than in most other conversations. We are challenged to listen more carefully and approach different points of view by looking at the deeper values and issues underlying them.

EIGHT PRINCIPLES FOR ENTERING INTO CONTEMPLATIVE DIALOGUE

1. Keep in mind that *Bridges* focuses on our "lived experience" and how the session theme connects to everyday life. Keep your comments rooted in your own experience and refrain from remarks that are overly abstract, philosophical, or theoretical.

2. Express your own thoughts knowing they will be heard to be reflected on and not necessarily responded to verbally. It is helpful to use "I" statements like "I believe . . ." or "I am confused by that response." Try framing your remarks with phrases such as "My assumption is that . . ." or "My experience has been . . ."

3. Pay attention to the assumptions, attitudes, and experiences underlying your initial or surface thoughts on the topic. Ask yourself questions like: "Why am I drawn to this particular part of the reading?" "What makes me feel this way?"

4. Remember to listen first and refrain from thinking about how you might respond to another's comments. Simply listen to and accept his or her thoughts on the subject without trying to challenge, critique, or even respond aloud to them.

5. Trust the group. Observe how the participants' ideas, reflections, common concerns, assumptions, and attitudes come together and form a collective group mind.

6. Reflect before speaking and be concise. Make one point or relate one experience then stop and allow others to do the same.

7. Expect periods of silence during the dialogue. Learn to be comfortable with the silence and resist the urge to speak just because there is silence.

8. In time you will adjust to saying something and not receiving a response and to listening without asking a question, challenging, or responding directly. Simply speaking to the theme or idea from your own experience or perspective takes some practice. Be patient with yourself and the other members of your group and watch for deepening levels of dialogue.

ADDITIONAL RESOURCES

A *Leader's Guide* for the *Bridges* series is available from Ave Maria Press.

Online resources available at www.avemariapress.com include:
- Leader's Guide
- Series Sampler
- Suggested Retreat Schedule
- Program Evaluation Form
- Links to other books about Thomas Merton
- Interview with Robert Toth of The Merton Institute for Contemplative Living
- www.mertoninstitute.org

Merton: A Film Biography (1 hour) provides an excellent overview on Merton's life and spiritual journey. The DVD version contains an additional hour of insights from those who knew him.

Contemplation and Action is a periodic newsletter from The Merton Institute with information about new Merton publications, programs, and events. It is free and can be obtained by visiting the Institute's website or calling 1-800-886-7275.

The Thomas Merton Spiritual Development Program is a basic introduction to Merton's life and his insights on contemplative spirituality, social justice, and inter-religious dialogue. Especially designed for youth, it includes a participant's workbook/journal.

WEEKLY MERTON REFLECTIONS

To receive a brief reflection from Merton's works via e-mail each week register at The Merton Institute website www.mertoninstitute.org or by contacting:

The Merton Institute for Contemplative Living
2117 Payne Street
Louisville, KY 40206
1-800-886-7275

session one

NATURE'S WISDOM FOR CONTEMPLATIVE LIVING

OPENING REFLECTION
FROM PSALM 119

> It was your hands that made me and shaped me;
> help me to learn your commands.
> Your faithful will see me and rejoice
> for I trust in your word.

INTRODUCTION TO THE TEXTS

No human being is an island: we are embedded from our mothers' wombs within a glorious ecology of kindness with every other being on Earth. God has willed us to live naturally in a matrix of dependent relationships. God is the beautiful spider who webs us to connection with every line of His creation. God is the mother of the ultimate website.

This paradise of connectedness to all other beings is all around us but we do not attend. We are too busy. Our lives have too many purposes. We miss the beauty all around us, wearing the blinders of stress and inattention as we rush from one situation to another. And all the while, we are being called to acknowledge the beauty of God's web of relationships into which all of us were born. We must learn to attend.

Merton's Voice

FROM *CONJECTURES OF A GUILTY BYSTANDER*

The first chirps of the waking birds mark the *"point vierge"* ["the virgin point"] of the dawn under a sky as yet without real light, a moment of awe and inexpressible innocence, when the Father in perfect silence opens their eyes. They begin to speak to Him, not with fluent song, but with an awakening question that is their dawn state, their state at the *"point vierge."* Their condition asks if it is time for them to "be." He answers, "Yes." Then, they one by one wake up and become birds. They manifest themselves as birds, beginning to sing. Presently they will be fully themselves, and will even fly.

Meanwhile, the most wonderful moment of the day is that when creation in its innocence asks permission to "be" once again, as it did on the first morning that ever was.

All wisdom seeks to collect and manifest itself at that blind sweet point. Man's wisdom does not succeed, for we are fallen into self-mastery and cannot ask permission of anyone. We face our mornings as men of undaunted purpose. We know the time and we dictate terms. We are in a position to dictate terms, we suppose: we have a clock that proves we are right from the very start. We know what time it is. We are in touch with the hidden inner laws. We will say in advance what kind of day it has to be. Then, if necessary, we will take steps to make it meet our requirements.

For the birds there is not a time that they tell, but the virgin point between darkness and light, between nonbeing and being. You can tell yourself the time by their waking, if you are experienced. But that is your folly, not theirs. Worse folly still if you think they are telling you something you might find useful—that it is, for example, four o'clock.

So they wake: first the catbirds and cardinals and some that I do not know. Later the song sparrows and the wrens. Last of all the doves and crows.

The waking of crows is most like the waking of men: querulous, noisy, and raw.

Here is an unspeakable secret: paradise is all around us and we do not understand. It is wide open. The sword is taken away, but we do not know it: we are off "one to his farm and another to his merchandise." Lights on. Clocks ticking. Thermostats working. Stoves cooking. Electric shavers filling radios with static. "Wisdom," cries the dawn deacon, but we do not attend (pp. 131–132).

ANOTHER VOICE
JOHN STEVENS, TRANSLATOR.
ONE ROBE, ONE BOWL: THE ZEN POETRY OF RYOKAN

> My hut lies in the middle of a dense forest;
> Every year the green ivy grows longer.
> No news of the affairs of men,
> Only the occasional song of a woodcutter.
> The sun shines and I mend my robe;
> When the moon comes out I read Buddhist poems.
> I have nothing to report, my friends.
> If you want to find the meaning, stop chasing after so many things.

—p. 43

Reflect and Dialogue

Which images, words, or phrases in these readings resonate most with your experience?

How do they make you feel?

What do they mean for your life?

Does nature play a significant role in your spiritual life?

How do you attend to the web of life of which we all are an intricate part?

Have you been able to "stop chasing after so many things?" If so, to what good end?

Why is morning so important a time for living contemplatively?

Closing

Conclude with one of the meditations on pages 51–52 or with a period of quiet reflection.

session two
CONTEMPLATION AS "VIRGIN TIME"

OPENING REFLECTION
FROM PSALM 119

> I have not turned from your decrees;
> you yourself have taught me.
> Your promise is sweeter to my taste
> than honey in the mouth.

INTRODUCTION TO THE TEXTS

We often choose to waste our valuable time. Losing a taste for leisure and rest, we often can't find our way back to that place in our hearts where time is redeemed by accepting our life as gift. When we live contemplatively, we allow our hearts to be attuned to the more balanced rhythms of life to which we otherwise seldom dance. We recover time by slowing down to appreciate the life we have been given as time to love and serve God and neighbor.

Contemplative living, Merton knew, could give us back time as "a space of liberty" where our hearts open out with their more simple prayers. Accepting time as our opportunity to be human and free (Christ has made us so), we grow more conscious of our birthright: we are alive and happiest when we pray.

When we live in time for God, God lives through time for us. Choosing moments when we dance through time, overcoming the times we only sweat through time, everything we experience becomes food for our minds and hearts. Like birds we have time to eat continually from God's open beak. Attending to time in prayer, God attends to us in time.

MERTON'S VOICE
FROM *THE OTHER SIDE OF THE MOUNTAIN*

The contemplative life must provide an area, a space of liberty, of silence, in which possibilities are allowed to surface and new choices—beyond routine choice—become manifest. It should create a new experience of time, not as stopgap, stillness, but as "*temps vierge*" ["virgin time"]—not a blank to be filled or an untouched space to be conquered and violated, but a space that can enjoy its own potentialities and hopes—its own presence to itself. One's own time, but not dominated by one's own ego and its demands. Hence open to others—*compassionate* time, rooted in the sense of common illusion and in criticism of it (p. 262).

ANOTHER VOICE
SOGYAL RINPOCHE, *THE TIBETAN BOOK OF LIVING AND DYING*

In trying really to listen, I have often been inspired by the Zen master Suzuki-roshi, who said: "If your mind is empty, it is always ready for anything; it is open to everything. In the beginner's mind there are many possibilities, in the expert's mind there are few." The beginner's mind is an open mind, an empty mind, a ready mind, and if we really listen with a beginner's mind, we might really begin to hear. For if we listen with a silent mind, as free as possible from the clamor of preconceived ideas, a possibility will be created for the truth of the teachings to pierce us, and for the meaning of life and death to become increasingly and startlingly clear. My master Dilgo Kysentse Rinpoche said: "The more and more you listen, the more and more you hear; the more and more you hear, the deeper and deeper your understanding becomes."

The deepening of understanding, then, comes through *contemplation* and reflection, the second tool of wisdom. As we contemplate what we have heard, it gradually begins to permeate our mindstream and saturate our inner experience of our lives. Everyday events start to mirror and more and more subtly and directly to confirm the truths of the teachings, as contemplation slowly unfolds and enriches what we have begun to understand intellectually and carries that understanding down from our head to our heart." (p. 122)

Reflect and Dialogue

Which images, words, or phrases in these readings resonate most with your experience?

How do they make you feel?

What do they mean for your life?

How do you relate to the concept of time?

Do you ever experience time as "virgin time"?

Are there special "places" where you feel freer?

Where are you more aware of your heart's deepest desires?

When are you most contemplative?

Closing

Conclude with one of the meditations on pages 51–52 or with a period of quiet reflection.

session three
OUR POOR SELVES
AND GOD'S MERCY

OPENING REFLECTION
FROM PSALM 119

> I yearn for your saving help;
> I hope in your word.
> My eyes yearn to see your promise.
> When will you console me?

INTRODUCTION TO THE TEXTS

We are consistently unfaithful to our vocation of discovering our most profoundly true identities in conscious relationship with God and neighbor. Our common unfaithfulness to this "one word of truth" (Ryokan)—that we were born to love one another, is a sorrowful mystery in everyone's journey of life. None of us actually comprehend our choices not to love, but step by conscious and unconscious steps, we find ourselves regularly deprived of a more natural facility to live out of, and speak out of, "our truth."

To love one another and God, and thus to find and love our true selves, is a consistently fragile enterprise. Our failures cause our tears. Merton advises, however, that we regard even our inexplicable failures to be true to ourselves with compassion, for "all that is poor deserves mercy."

FROM *NEW SEEDS OF CONTEMPLATION*

The presence of God in His world as its Creator depends on no one but Him. His presence in the world as Man depends, in some measure, upon men. Not that we can do anything to change the mystery of the Incarnation in itself: but we are able to decide whether we ourselves, and that portion of the world which is ours, shall become aware of His presence, consecrated by it, and transfigured in its light.

We have the choice of two identities: the external mask which seems to be real and which lives by a shadowy autonomy for the brief moment of earthly existence, and the hidden, inner person who seems to be nothing, but who can give himself eternally to the truth in which he subsists. It is this inner self that is taken up into the mystery of Christ, by His love, by the Holy Spirit, so that in secret we live "in Christ."

Yet we must not deal in too negative a fashion even with the "external self." This self is not by nature evil, and the fact that it is unsubstantial is not to be imputed to it as some kind of crime. It is afflicted with metaphysical poverty: but all that is poor deserves mercy. So too our outward self: as long as it does not isolate itself in a lie, it is blessed by the mercy and the love of Christ. Appearances are to be accepted for what they are. The accidents of a poor and transient existence have, nevertheless, an ineffable value. They can be transparent media in which we apprehend the presence of God in the world. It is possible to speak of the exterior self as a mask: to do so is not necessarily to reprove it. The mask that each man wears may well be a disguise not only for that man's inner self but also for God, wandering as a pilgrim and exile in his own creation.

And indeed, if Christ became Man, it is because He wanted to be any man and every man. If we believe in the Incarnation of the Son of God, there should be no one on earth in whom we are not prepared to see, in mystery, the presence of Christ (pp. 295–296).

ANOTHER VOICE
LEONARD COHEN, *STRANGER MUSIC*

"You Who Pour Mercy Into Hell"

You who pour mercy into hell, sole authority in the highest and the lowest worlds, let your anger disperse the mist in this aimless place, where even my sins fall short of the mark. Let me be with you again, absolute companion; let me study your ways which are just beyond the hope of evil. Seize my heart out of its fantasy; direct my mind from the fiction of secrecy, you who know the secrets of every heart, whose mercy is to be the secret of longing. Let every heart declare its secret, let every song disclose your love; let us bring to you the sorrows of our freedom. Blessed are you, who open a gate, in every moment, to enter in truth or tarry in hell. Let me be with you again, let me put this away, you who wait beside me, who have broken down your world to gather hearts. Blessed is your name; blessed is the confession of your name. Kindle the darkness of my calling; let me cry to the one who judges the heart in justice and mercy. Arouse my heart again with the limitless breath you breathe into me, arouse the secret from obscurity (p. 325).

Reflect and Dialogue

Which images, words, or phrases in these readings resonate most with your experience?

How do they make you feel?

What do they mean for your life?

How would you describe your "inner self"? What about your "external self"?

Have you ever considered that the masks you wear might disguise God? What implications does this assertion of Merton's have for you?

How have you experienced the mercy of God?

Closing

Conclude with one of the meditations on pages 51–52 or with a period of quiet reflection.

session four
BEING CONTEMPLATIVE
IS LEARNING TO LIVE

OPENING REFLECTION
FROM PSALM 119

> Your word is a lamp for my steps
> and a light for my path.
> I have sworn and have made up my mind
> to obey your decrees.

INTRODUCTION TO THE TEXTS

One way of regarding the discipline of contemplative dialogue that we have taken up together is that we are making an attempt to speak with our most authentic voices. We are learning to speak from our hearts and minds just as they are without fear of recrimination or facing argument. Our real voice has always been waiting to sound itself above the voices of our parents, of our teachers, of our cultures. In contemplative dialogue, we are educating ourselves to speak authentically, to say our deepest "yes" and our deepest "no."

Merton once compared his deepest self with a "wild, shy deer" that only makes an appearance when it knows it is safe. In contemplative dialogue we are teaching one another to speak with integrity in the safety of our attempts to hear deeply what each of us truly has to say. Paraphrasing the Canadian poet Leonard Cohen, as we dialogue contemplatively, we are "stuttering together to make our truest words flesh."

MERTON'S VOICE
FROM "LEARNING TO LIVE" IN *LOVE AND LIVING*

Life consists in learning to live on one's own, spontaneous, freewheeling: to do this one must recognize what is one's own—be familiar and at home with oneself. This means basically learning who one is, and learning what one has to offer to the contemporary world, and then learning how to make that offering valid.

The purpose of education is to show us how to define ourselves authentically and spontaneously in relation to our world—not to impose a prefabricated definition of the world, still less an arbitrary definition of ourselves as individuals. The world is made up of the people who are fully alive in it: that is, of the people who can be themselves in it and can enter into a living and fruitful relationship with each other in it. The world is, therefore, more real in proportion as the people in it are able to be more fully and more humanly alive: that is to say, better able to make a lucid and conscious use of their freedom. Basically, this freedom must consist first of all in the capacity to choose their own lives, to find themselves on the deepest possible level. A superficial freedom to wander aimlessly here and there, to taste this or that, to make a choice of distractions (in Pascal's sense [*divertissement*]) is simply a sham. It claims to be a freedom of "choice" when it has evaded the basic task of discovering who it is that chooses. It is not free because it is unwilling to face the risk of self-discovery.

The function of the university is, then first of all, to help students discover themselves: to recognize themselves, and to identify who it is that chooses.

27

This description will be recognized at once as unconventional and, in fact, monastic. To put it in even more outrageous terms, the function of the university is to help men and women save their souls and, in so doing, to save their society: from what? From the hell of meaninglessness, of obsession, of complex artifice, of systematic lying, of criminal evasions and neglects, of self-destructive futilities.

It will be evident from my context that the business of saving one's soul means more than taking an imaginary object, "a soul," and entrusting it to some institutional bank for deposit until it is recovered with interest in heaven (pp. 3–4).

ANOTHER VOICE
THOMAS DEL PRETE, *THOMAS MERTON AND THE EDUCATION OF THE WHOLE PERSON*

The origin of voice is interior, its quality subjective in that it expresses a deeply personal experience of something known. The existential and relational nature of this personal experience reflects an epistemology [a way of knowing] grounded in the reality of being, in one's being united to truth and living reality in the fullness of being, that is, in the hidden wholeness and love of God. The voice of the whole person will be authentic in proportion as it emerges from and expresses this whole quality of knowing. This implies a certain quality of innocence on the part of the person. To speak authentically and thus innocently, the whole person must speak in humble fidelity and response to life, person, and reality; one must strive to speak from an integrity of openness and honest response to a deep, interior experience of knowing the truth or apprehending reality. The "external" words which one voices are as much as possible formulated in conformity to the "interior" words which express one's personal experience in relation to truth or reality; as Merton says, they are the unique, creative expression of "me" (the whole person) in relation to a situation. The effort to speak in accordance with genuine interior response will be a vital sign of the quality of personal communication involved in the formation of the whole person (p. 124).

REFLECT AND DIALOGUE

Which images, words, or phrases in these readings resonate most with your experience?

How do they make you feel?

What do they mean for your life?

In what ways, through contemplative dialogue, are you becoming freer to "choose your own life" and to "find yourself on the deepest possible level"?

How is this practice of contemplative dialogue helping you speak with "the voice of your whole person"? How has it changed the quality of your personal communication?

CLOSING

Conclude with one of the meditations on pages 51–52 or with a period of quiet reflection.

session five
FINDING OUR
OWN SOULS

OPENING REFLECTION
FROM PSALM 119

> Blessed are you, O Lord;
> teach me your statutes.
> With my tongue I have recounted
> the decrees of your lips.
> I rejoice to do your will
> as though all riches were mine.

INTRODUCTION TO THE TEXTS

To live out of our own souls, to sound to others the words our souls speak, is the ripening of our "mature identities." Our most personal identities reveal themselves when we set aside the masks we wear and the roles we are forced to play. Within these moments of being without disguise we hear again the words that God has been speaking to us since our births.

Merton wrote of a "virgin point" within us where God loves us and is always speaking to us to come out and "be." Through our inner work of contemplative prayer, we are educating ourselves to receive from God the revelation of our heart's virginity. We learn through contemplation "to sit still and be what we have become."

"Learning to be oneself means learning to die in order to live." We are continually learning how to be ourselves and God is continually calling us to rise from death to greater life and joy.

Merton's Voice
From "Learning to Live" in *Love and Living*

Speaking as a Christian existentialist, I mean by "soul" not simply the Aristotelian essential form but the mature personal identity, the creative fruit of an authentic and lucid search. [I mean] the "self" that is found after other partial and exterior selves have been discarded as masks.

This metaphor must not mislead: this inner identity is not "found" as an object, but is the very self that finds. It is lost when it forgets to find, when it does not know how to seek, or when it seeks itself as an object. (Such a search is futile and self-contradictory.) Hence the paradox that it finds best when it stops seeking, and the graduate level of learning is when one learns to sit still and be what one has become, which is what one does not know and does not need to know. In the language of Sufism, the end of the ascetic life is *Rida*, satisfaction. Debts are paid (and they were largely imaginary). One no longer seeks something else. One no longer seeks to be told by another who one is. One no longer demands reassurance. But there is the whole infinite depth of *what* is remaining to be revealed. And it is not revealed to those who seek it from others.

Education in this sense means more than learning; and for such education, one is awarded no degree. One graduates by rising from the dead. Learning to be oneself means, therefore, learning to die in order to live. It means discovering in the ground of one's being a "self" which is ultimate and indestructible, which not only survives the destruction of all other more superficial selves, but finds its identity affirmed and clarified by their destruction (pp. 4–5).

ANOTHER VOICE

EKNATH EASWARAN, TRANSLATOR, *THE DHAMMAPADA*

The Saint.

He has completed his voyage; he has gone beyond sorrow. The fetters of life have fallen from him, and he lives in full freedom.

The thoughtful strive always. They have no fixed abode, but leave home like swans from their lake.

Like the flight of birds in the sky, it is hard to follow the path of the selfless. They have no possessions, but live on alms in a world of freedom. Like the flight of birds in the sky, it is hard to follow their path. With their senses under control, temperate in eating, they know the meaning of freedom.

Wisdom has stilled their minds, and their thoughts, words and deeds are filled with peace. Freed from illusion and from personal ties, they have renounced the world of appearances to find reality. Thus have they reached the highest.

They make holy wherever they dwell, in village or forest, on land or at sea. With their senses at peace and minds full of joy, they make the forests holy (pp. 102–103).

Reflect and Dialogue

Which images, words, or phrases in these readings resonate most with your experience?

How do they make you feel?

What do they mean for your life?

Merton writes, "One graduates by rising from the dead." How has "learning to die in order to live" been part of your life's education?

Has there been a particular time in your life when you learned "to sit still and be what [you have] become"?

Who is a "saint" to you? What is "sanctity"?

Closing

Conclude with one of the meditations on pages 51–52 or with a period of quiet reflection.

session six

THE TRANSPARENT HOLINESS OF OUR EVERYDAY LIVES

OPENING REFLECTION
FROM PSALM 119

> Lord, let your love come upon me,
> the saving help of your promise. . . .
> Do not take the word of truth from my mouth
> for I trust in your decrees.
> I shall always keep your law
> forever and ever.
> I shall walk in the path of freedom
> for I seek your precepts.

INTRODUCTION TO THE TEXTS

When Merton was unripe in his contemplative life, he considered the gate to his monastery as the gate to paradise. As Merton matured in his contemplative life, he realized that the "gate of heaven is everywhere." The gate to paradise appears locked to us whenever we turn our faces down to focus on our own needs and cares, the limited concerns of "my life, my family, and my work." The gate to paradise is seen wide open whenever we raise our eyes to take in everything and everyone around us.

Compassion and self-forgetfulness open the gates to a paradise of unity with all beings with whom we are sharing time. In the moments we forget ourselves and "join in the General Dance," as Merton wrote in *New Seeds of Contemplation*, everything in our lives becomes transparent with love and is seen in a new light. Everyone and everything around us becomes precious, as they always were, but we did not realize the treasure before us. We did not make the effort to see. Let us awake from our slumbering. "We are living in a world that is absolutely transparent, and God is shining through it all the time."

MERTON'S VOICE
FROM "A LIFE FREE FROM CARE"

Let us face the fact for once that what we are here for is love. And what is love? When you love another person you simply forget yourself and think about the other person. You are not concerned with yourself. And if you love this other person and know that it is mutual then you know the other person is thinking about you. So that what happens in love is that each one forgets himself in order to live in and through the other. This is what God asks of us. He asks us to live in such a way that we don't have to think about ourselves, He will think about us. So you are no longer worrying about whether you are virtuous or not, you just live. You live without care and without concern for anything of yourself.

Now what this does—and I know, from what experience I have of it so far, it *does*—is that in fact it is sometimes possible to see that things become transparent. They are no longer opaque, and they no longer hide God. This is true. The thing that we have to face is that life is as simple as this: We are living in a world that is absolutely transparent, and

God is shining through it all the time. This is not just a fable or a nice story; it is true. And this is something we are not able to see. But when we abandon ourselves to Him and forget ourselves, we see it sometimes and we see it maybe frequently: that God manifests Himself everywhere, in everything—in people and in things and in nature and in events and so forth. So that it becomes very obvious that God is everywhere, He is in everything, and we cannot be without Him. You cannot be without God. It's impossible; it's just simply impossible. The only thing is that we don't see it. This again is what we are here for.

What is it that makes the world opaque? It is care. Everything becomes opaque in proportion as we regard it as an individual object and become concerned with it. There is this individual thing; there is this day that I have to live through. It's a particular day, and so it's opaque. It comes to me in a big opaque package and I spend my time opening it up. And then when I have taken all of the package apart, it's the evening, it's the examination of conscience and I examine myself: and I took all the paper off the package and there *wasn't anything in it.* Then the next day comes along, and that is what we do again. Until a big event comes—I don't know—I get the job of teaching something to the rabbits. It becomes a great thing, and I take the paper off this, piece by piece by piece, and then there's nothing in that either. So you have to leave the rabbits what they are, rabbits; and, if you can see that they are rabbits, you suddenly see that they are transparent, and that the humanity of God is transparent in people. And that you don't have to take each person as an opaque package. "Who is the mystery of this crazy person here that I have to analyze?" and I look across the choir: "What makes that guy tick?" You don't have to know what makes the man tick. All you have to see is that he is a manifestation of the humanity of God. There is humaneness, humanness, *manness* in God, which is manifested in every human being: not only by the fact that we are creatures of God but by the fact that we are redeemed in Christ. This again is our life, and this is what it is for (pp. 221–222).

ANOTHER VOICE
OLIVIER CLÉMENT, *THE ROOTS OF CHRISTIAN MYSTICISM*

Spiritual progress has no other test in the end, nor any better expression, than our ability to love. It has to be unselfish love founded on respect, a service, a disinterested affection that does not ask to be paid in return, a "sympathy," indeed an "empathy" that takes us out of ourselves enabling us to "feel with" the other person and indeed to "feel in" him or her. It gives us the ability to discover in the other person an inward nature as mysterious and deep as our own, but different and willed to be so by God.

In this fallen world the unity of human beings has been broken, everything is a "rat race," and I try to free myself from the anguish that torments me by projecting it on another, the scapegoat of my tragic finiteness. The other person is always my enemy and I need him to be so. In Christ, however, death has been defeated, my inner hell transformed into the Church, I no longer need to have enemies, no one is separated from anyone. The criterion of the depth of one's spiritual growth is therefore love for one's enemies, in accordance with the paradoxical commandment of the Gospel that takes its meaning solely from the cross—Christ's cross and ours—and from the resurrection—again Christ's and our own. . . .

The true miracle, the most difficult achievement, is therefore the example and practice of love in the spiritual sense of that word (and here the Gospel speaks of *agape*, the Latin *caritas*). To enter into God is to let oneself be caught up in the immense movement of the love of the Trinity which reveals the other person to us as "neighbor" or (and this is better) which enables each one of us to become the "neighbor" of others. And to become a "neighbor" is to side with Christ, since he identifies himself with every human being who is suffering, or rejected, or imprisoned, or ignored (pp. 270–271).

REFLECT AND DIALOGUE

Which images, words, or phrases in these readings resonate most with your experience?

How do they make you feel?

What do they mean for your life?

At what moments in your own life has the world become transparent and God was shining through everyone and everything you encountered?

How do you strive to be a neighbor to all whom you encounter?

What keeps you from experiencing the face of God in all things?

CLOSING

Conclude with one of the meditations on pages 51–52 or with a period of quiet reflection.

session seven

BECOMING GOD'S BOOK FOR EVERYONE TO READ

OPENING REFLECTION
FROM PSALM 119

> Your word, O Lord, forever
> stands firm in the heavens:
> your truth lasts from age to age,
> like the earth you created.
> By your decree it endures to this day;
> for all things serve you.

INTRODUCTION

Nothing is more precious and revelatory of God than the face of a human being. The human face reveals and signifies the person. It is the locus of our recognizing one another. Our faces, for those who love us, are unforgettable symbols of everything our person means for them.

We speak of being able or of being unable to read someone's face. We speak of reading some faces as if they were open books. Merton's contemplative vision was to realize that all human faces he encountered were potentially "open books" for him. Each face, read carefully with love, spoke to him of Christ.

Merton's contemplative living was incarnational. At the end of the day, the fruit of all contemplative living is love enacted for others, *caritas,* which Merton called the "love that brings us back to all the others in one Christ."

MERTON'S VOICE
FROM *THE SEARCH FOR SOLITUDE*

[In Louisville, I bought some] marvelous books for a few pennies—including *The Family of Man* for fifty cents. All those fabulous pictures. And again, no refinements and no explanations are necessary! How scandalized some would be if I said that the whole book is to me a picture of Christ, and yet that is the Truth. There, there is Christ in my own Kind, my own Kind—"Kind" which means "likeness" and which means "love" and which means "child." Humankind. Like one another, the dear "Kind" of sinners united and embraced in only one heart, in only one Kindness, which is the Heart and Kindness of Christ. I do not look for sin in you, Humankind. I do not see sin in you anymore today (though we are all sinners). There is something too real to allow sin any longer to seem important, to seem to exist, for it has been swallowed up, sin has been destroyed, it is gone, and there is only the great secret between us that we are all one Kind and what matters is not what this or that one has committed in his heart, separate from the others, but the love that brings us back to all the others in one Christ, and their love is not our love but the Divine Bridegroom's. It is the Divine Power and the divine Joy—and God is seen and reveals himself as man, human, that is in us, and there is no other hope of finding wisdom than in God-manhood: our own manhood transformed in God (pp. 182–183).

ANOTHER VOICE
MEVLÂNA JALÂLUDDIN RUMI IN *JEWELS OF REMEMBRANCE*

During Prayer I am accustomed to turn to God
like this
And recall the meaning of the words of the
Tradition,
"the delight felt in the ritual prayer." **
The window of my soul opens,
and from the purity of the unseen world,
the book of God comes to me straight.
The book, the rain of divine grace, and the light
are falling into my house through a window
from my real and original source.
The house without a window is hell;
to make a window is the essence of true religion.
Don't thrust your ax upon every thicket;
come, use your ax to cut open a window.

**The Prophet Muhammad (peace and blessings be upon him) is said to have mentioned this as one of the three things he loved best in the world [Translators] (p.22).

REFLECT AND DIALOGUE

Which images, words, or phrases in these readings resonate most with your experience?

How do they make you feel?

What do they mean for your life?

Whose faces have revealed God's face to you?

How have you been able to open the window of your soul so that the "book of God" can come to you?

Why would His Holiness the Dalai Lama have written that his religion is "kindness"?

CLOSING

Conclude with one of the meditations on pages 51–52 or with a period of quiet reflection.

session eight
DISCOVERING THE HIDDEN GROUND OF LOVE

> Your will is wonderful indeed;
> therefore, I obey it.
> The unfolding of your word gives light
> and teaches the simple.
> I open my mouth and I sigh
> as I yearn for your commands.
> Turn and show me your mercy;
> show justice to your friend.

INTRODUCTION TO THE TEXTS

In *New Seeds of Contemplation,* Merton wrote that our true identities are hidden in God. We shall never cease discovering who we are because we shall never cease discovering who God is for us. Gregory of Nyssa, a Christian theologian of the fourth century, wrote that our discovery of the mystery of God's love for us would not cease even after we die. Gregory asserted that we would spend eternity discovering the deeper epiphanies of our identities in the light of God's continually renewed and all-encompassing love for us.

It is truly futile, then, for us to want to name precisely who it is we truly are. We will never be capable of having our names spelled out for us by others or even by ourselves. We shall always be mysteries to ourselves and to one another.

In this passage from his journals, Merton designs a metaphor for our understanding the hidden-ness of our identities. He had had a visit from one of his life's best teachers, Columbia professor and poet Mark Van Doren. As they walked in the woods, Van Doren reminded Merton, "The birds don't know they have names."

Within each of us is a mirror that reflects the secret of God's own nameless identity. Although we enjoy the attempt to name God, every bird, and ourselves, we shall never fully know—even in eternity—the NAME under God's names, or our own NAME hidden under all our names.

The quest for our identities in God and for God's identity in us has no end. This truth should not render us restless and disappointed, for it allows us, once we apprehend it, to rejoice. Our search for the deepest identity of God as Love for us, and for our deepest identities as Love for God, will never cease.

MERTON'S VOICE
FROM *A SEARCH FOR SOLITUDE*

The warblers are coming through now. Very hard to identify them all, even with field glasses and a bird book. (Have seen at least one that is definitely not in the bird book.) Watching one that I took to be a Tennessee warbler. A beautiful, neat, prim little thing—seeing this beautiful thing which people do not usually see, looking into this world of birds, which is not concerned with us or with our problems, I felt very close to God or felt religious anyway. Watching those birds was as food for meditation, or as mystical reading. Perhaps better.

Also the beautiful, unidentified red flower or fruit I found on a bud yesterday. These things say so much more than words.

Mark Van Doren, when he was here, said, "The birds don't know they have names."

Watching them I thought: who cares what they are called? But do I have the courage not to care? Why not be like Adam, in a new world of my own, and call them by my own names?

That would still mean that I thought the names were important.

No name and no word to identify the beauty and reality of those birds today is the gift of God to me in letting me see them.

(And that name—God—is not a name! It is like a letter X or Y. Yahweh is a better Name—it finally means Nameless One) (pp. 123–124).

ANOTHER VOICE
GREGORY OF NYSSA, "HOMILIES ON THE BEATITUDES"

"The kingdom of God is within you" (Luke 17:21). From this we learn that by a heart made pure . . . we see in our own beauty the image of the godhead . . . You have in you the ability to see God. He who formed you put in your being an immense power. When God created you he enclosed in you the image of his perfection, as the mark of a seal is imposed on wax. But your straying has obscured God's image . . . you are like a metal coin: on the whetstone the rust disappears. The coin was dirty, but now it reflects the brightness of the sun and shines in its turn. Like the coin, the inward part of the personality, called the heart by our Master, once rid of the rust that hid its beauty, will rediscover the first likeness and be real . . . So when people look at themselves they will see in themselves the One they are seeking. And this is the joy that will fill their purified hearts. They are looking at their own translucency and find the model in the image. When the sun is looked at in a mirror, even without any raising of the eyes to heaven, the sun's brightness is seen in the mirror exactly as if the sun's disc itself were being looked at. You cannot contemplate the reality of the light; but if you rediscover the beauty of the image that was put in you at the beginning, you will obtain within yourself the goal of your desires. . . . The divine image will shine brightly in us in Christ Jesus our Lord, to whom be glory throughout the ages (p. 237).

Reflect and Dialogue

Which images, words, or phrases in these readings resonate most with your experience?

How do they make you feel?

What do they mean for your life?

Gregory of Nyssa says that we are "like a metal coin: on the whetstone the rust disappears." What have been the whetstones in your life? What has helped you rid your inner being of its spiritual rust? What are your life's personal names for God?

If you were free to give yourself a name, other than the beautiful name you were born with, whom would you want to be called?

Closing

Conclude with one of the meditations on pages 51–52 or with a period of quiet reflection.

CONCLUDING MEDITATIONS

A.

My Lord God,
I have no idea where I am going. I do not see the road ahead of me. I cannot know for certain where it will end. Nor do I really know myself, and the fact that I think I am following your will does not mean that I am actually doing so. But I believe that the desire to please you does in fact please you. And I hope I have that desire in all that I am doing. I hope that I will never do anything apart from that desire. And I know that, if I do this, you will lead me by the right road, though I may know nothing about it. Therefore I will trust you always though I may seem to be lost and in the shadow of death. I will not fear, for you are ever with me, and you will never leave me to face my perils alone.

Thomas Merton
Thoughts in Solitude, p. 83

B.

When the soul, at the call of its beloved, goes out to look for him whom no name can reach, it learns . . . . that it is enamored of one who is inaccessible, and is desirous of one who cannot be grasped. These words strike the soul and wound it with despair, because it believes its search for fullness will never come to an end . . . . But the veil of its sadness is taken away from it when it is taught that to go forward continually in its search, and never to cease raising its sights, constitutes the true enjoyment of what it desires. Each time its desire is fulfilled, the desire for higher realities is engendered.

Gregory of Nyssa,
"Sermons on the Song of Songs,"
12 *Patrologia Graeca* 44, pp. 1036–37

C.

This is what it means to seek God perfectly:
to withdraw
from illusion and pleasure,
from worldly anxieties and desires,
from the works that God does not want,
from a glory that is only human display;
to keep my mind free from confusion in order that
    my liberty may be always at the disposal of His will;
to entertain silence in my heart and listen for the
    voice of God.

And then to wait in peace and emptiness and oblivion
    of all things.

Thomas Merton
New Seeds of Contemplation, pp. 44–46, excerpted

SOURCES

The readings from the Psalms are from *The Psalms*. Arranged by Joseph Gelineau. New York/Mahwah: Paulist Press, 1966.

FROM MERTON

A Search for Solitude. Journals, V.3. Lawrence S. Cunningham, ed. San Francisco: HarperSanFrancisco, 1996.

Conjectures of A Guilty Bystander. New York: Doubleday, 1966.

"A Life Free from Care." *Cistercian Studies* 5 (1970).

"Learning to Live" in *Love and Living*. Edited by Naomi Burton Stone and Brother Patrick Hart. New York: Farrar, Straus & Giroux, 1979.

New Seeds of Contemplation. New York: New Directions Press, 1961.

The Other Side of the Mountain, Journals Volume 7. Edited by Patrick Hart, OCSO. San Francisco: HarperSanFrancisco, 1999.

OTHER VOICES

Clément, Olivier. *The Roots of Christian Mysticism.* Hyde Park, New York: New City Press, 1993.

Cohen, Leonard. *Stranger Music: Selected Poems and Songs.* Toronto, Ontario: McClelland & Stewart Inc., 1993.

Del Prete, Thomas. *Thomas Merton and the Education of the Whole Person.* Birmingham, Alabama: Religious Education Press, 1990.

Easwaran, Eknath translator. *The Dhammapada.* Tomales, California: Nilgiri Press, 1985.

Gregory of Nyssa. "Homilies on the Beatitudes" and "Sermons on the Song of Songs." Quoted and translated in Olivier Clément, *The Roots of Christian Mysticism.* Hyde Park, New York: New City Press, 1993.

Helminski, Camille and Kabir translators. *Jewels of Remembrance: A Daybook of Spiritual Guidance Containing 365 Selections From the Wisdom of Mevlâna Jalâluddin Rumi.* Boston: Shambhala, 2000.

Rinpoche, Sogyal. *The Tibetan Book of Living and Dying.* Patrick Gaffney and Andrew Harvey, eds. SanFrancisco: HarperSanFrancisco, 1992.

Ryokan, Taigu. *One Robe, One Bowl: The Zen Poetry of Ryokan.* John Stevens, translator. New York: Weatherhill, 1977.

other voices

BIOGRAPHICAL SKETCHES

Olivier Clément is a French Orthodox theologian who has taught at St. Sergius Institute in Paris. In addition to his magisterial *The Roots of Christian Mysticism*, he has authored *Three Prayers: The Lord's Prayer, O Heavenly King, Prayer of Saint Ephrem*; *On Human Being: Spiritual Anthropology*; and *You Are Peter: An Orthodox Reflection on the Exercise of Papal Primacy*.

Leonard Norman Cohen is a Canadian poet, novelist, and singer-songwriter. Cohen began his career in literature, publishing his first book of poetry in Montreal in 1956 and his first novel in 1963. Following his breakthrough in the music industry in the late 1960s, Cohen became one of the most distinguished and influential songwriters of the late twentieth century.

Thomas Del Prete is Chair and Director of the Jacob Hiatt Center for Urban Education at Clark University in Worcester, Massachusetts. He is currently project director for the Carnegie "Schools for a New Society" systemic high school reform initiative in Worcester, as well as for federal Teach Quality Enhancement grants that promote the development of high quality urban teacher preparation and professional development.

Eknath Easwaran (1911–1999) was a successful writer, lecturer, and professor of English literature when he came to the United States on the Fulbright exchange program in 1959. Two years later he founded the Blue Mountain Center of Meditation in Berkeley, California. At the University of California, Berkeley, he taught what was probably the first credit course on the theory and practice of mediation to be offered at a major university in the West. He was prolific throughout his life in authoring books on meditation and spiritual practices within world contemplative traditions.

Gregory of Nyssa (c. 330–c. 395) is one of the great Cappadocian theologians. He authored classics of Christian mystical literature among which are *Homilies on the Song of Songs*, *Life of Moses*, and *On Love of the Poor*. In the words of Olivier Clément, "In the history of human thought Gregory appears as the one who broke the cycles of ancient thought, who rehabilitated becoming, who gave time a positive value as the apprenticeship of love, and supremely the one who showed that human beings have no other definition than to be indefinable, because they are made by God's infinitude and created for it" (*Roots of Christian Mysticism*, 339).

Mawlana Jalal ad-Din Muhammad Rumi (1207–1273), known to the English-speaking world simply as Rumi, was a Persian poet, jurist, theologian, and teacher of Sufism. Rumi's importance transcends national and ethnic borders. His poems have been translated into many languages and have appeared in various formats. He was also the founder of the Mevlevi order, better known as the

"Whirling Dervishes," who believe in performing their worship in the form of dance and music ceremony called the *sema*.

Sogyal Rinpoche was born in Tibet c. 1950 and educated in England where he studied Comparative Religion at Cambridge University. Author of the highly acclaimed *The Tibetan Book of Living and Dying*, he is one of the most renowned teachers of our time. He founded RIGPA, a Spiritual Care program that brings the wisdom and compassion of his teachings to professional and trained volunteers who work in end-of-life care.

Taigu Ryokan (1758–1831), nicknamed Great Fool, lives on as one of Japan's best loved poets, the wise fool who wrote of his humble life with much directness. He had no disciples, ran no temple, and in the eyes of the world was a penniless monk who spent his life in the snow country of Mt. Kugami. He admired most the Soto Zen teachings of Dogen Zenji and the unconventional life and poetry of Zen mountain poet Han-shan. He repeatedly refused to be honored or confined as a "professional" either as a Buddhist priest or a poet. His practice consisted of sitting in *zazen* meditation, walking in the woods, playing with children, making his daily begging rounds, reading and writing poetry, doing calligraphy, and on occasion drinking wine with friends (Yakrider.com).

about

THE EDITORS

The Merton Institute for Contemplative Living is dedicated to personal spiritual transformation through raising awareness of Merton's spiritual insights and contemplative practices. Their purpose is to promote his vision for a just and peaceful world.

Robert G. Toth has served as the executive director of the Merton Institute since 1998. He is the editor of the *Contemplation and Action* newsletter and wrote the foreword to *Thomas Merton: An Introduction* by William H. Shannon.

Jonathan Montaldo is the associate director of The Merton Institute for Contemplative Living. He is the former director of the Thomas Merton Center at Bellarmine University and past president of the International Thomas Merton Society. Montaldo edited *Entering the Silence*, the *Merton Journals, Volume 2* (1996) and *The Intimate Merton: His Life from His Journals* (1999) with Br. Patrick Hart. He published *Dialogues with Silence: Thomas Merton's Prayers & Drawings* (2001); *Merton & Hesychasm: The Prayer of the Heart* (2003) and *A Year with Thomas Merton: Daily Reflections from His Journals* (2005).

Bridges to Contemplative Living with Thomas Merton

Bridges to Contemplative Living with Thomas Merton gently leads participants on a journey toward spiritual transformation and a mor contemplative and peace-filled life. Each eight-session booklet pro- vides an introduction to Merton and contemplative living through prayers, readings from Merton and other spiritual masters, and que: tions for small group dialogue.

Booklets in the Series

One
Entering the School of Your Experience
(Fall 2006)

Two
Becoming Who You Already Are
(Fall 2006)

Three
Living Your Deepest Desires
(Spring 2007)

Four
Discovering the Hidden Ground of Love
(Spring 2007)

Five
Traveling Your Road to Joy
(Fall 2007)

Six
Writing Yourself int the Book of Life
(Fall 2007)

Seven
Adjusting Your Life's Vision
(Spring 2008)

Eight
Seeing that Paradise Begins Now
(Spring 2008)

A FREE series Leader's Guide is available for download at www.avemariapress.com

Available from your bookstore or from
ave maria press / Notre Dame, IN 46556
www.avemariapress.com / Ph: 800-282-1865
A Ministry of the Indiana Province of Holy Cross

Keycode: FØAØ1Ø7ØØC